Mel Bay Presents

A Classic Christmas

Favorite Classical Tunes Combined with Familiar Carols

by Gail Smith

1 2 3 4 5 6 7 8 9 0

© 2005 BY MEL BAY PUBLICATIONS, INC., PACIFIC, MO 63069.
ALL RIGHTS RESERVED. INTERNATIONAL COPYRIGHT SECURED. B.M.I. MADE AND PRINTED IN U.S.A.
No part of this publication may be reproduced in whole or in part, or stored in a retrieval system, or transmitted in any form
or by any means, electronic, mechanical, photocopy, recording, or otherwise, without written permission of the publisher.

Visit us on the Web at www.melbay.com — E-mail us at email@melbay.com

Table of Contents

Joy to the World

Combined with Bach's Two-Part Invention in C

Arranged by Gail Smith

© 2005 Mel Bay Publications. All Rights Reserved.

4

5

The First Noel

Combined with Satie's Gymnopedie No. 1

Arranged by Gail Smith

© 2005 Mel Bay Publications. All Rights Reserved.

We Three Kings

Combined with Bach's Two-Part Invention in D minor

Arranged by Gail Smith

© 2005 Mel Bay Publications. All Rights Reserved.

9

God Rest Ye Merry Gentlemen

Combined with Bach's Two-Part Invention in A minor

Arranged by Gail Smith

© 2005 Mel Bay Publications. All Rights Reserved.

What Child is This

Combined with Beethoven's Für Elise

Arranged by Gail Smith

© 2005 Mel Bay Publications. All Rights Reserved.

16

mancando

It Came Upon a Midnight Clear

Combined with Chopin's Nocturne in E flat

Arranged by Gail Smith

© 2005 Mel Bay Publications. All Rights Reserved.

19

O Come O Come Emmanuel

Combined with Beethoven's Moonlight Sonata

Arranged by Gail Smith

© 2005 Mel Bay Publications. All Rights Reserved.

D.S. al Coda

23

The Shepherds at the Manger

Franz Liszt

© 2005 Mel Bay Publications. All Rights Reserved.

Pedal the first half of
each bar.

27

The March of the Magi
(Adeste Fidelis)

Franz Liszt

Tempo di Marcia moderato

© 2005 Mel Bay Publications. All Rights Reserved.

un poco accel.

ff